A Monster Chase

Summary & Analysis

This summarized version of "A Monster Chase" is not intended to replace the book but a complement for a better understanding of the problems at hand the author intended to show. This summary might also be useful for teachers of civil rights, law and healthcare policy.

Copyright

Edition: 1

ISBN-13: 978-0967064376

Part I

"After reading this book, one yearns for solutions."

Synopsis:

A young journalist, Anna Vitiello, confronted with the shortage of medical providers, investigates the disappearance of a physician she had known.

Anna uncovers concerning issues about the approach to the physician's disciplinary process. These findings bring in question our judiciary system and the harm done to healthcare.

Issues:

1. Does punishing medical providers resolve our healthcare financial crisis or aggravate the shortages of doctors?
2. Is our justice system effective?
3. Are abuses of power, acts of prosecutorial misconduct, or judicial oversights resulting in wrongful convictions or causing favoritism toward perpetrators?

Amana, Iowa

The protagonist, Anna Vitiello, lives in a typical small town in America where a tragedy has just occurred. A child died in the waiting area of a hospital's emergency room due to insufficient staffing.

A shortage of physicians has caused the death of the young girl. Meanwhile, Anna is unable to find a doctor to deliver her baby. These two events remind her of how her doctor disappeared where she went to college. She wonders whether the present scarcity might be the result of a larger problem. She decides to investigate the reason for the doctor's disappearance.

CHAPTER 1

Anna Vitiello, Dakota

In this chapter, we return to Anna's life in her college town where she courts Paul, her future spouse. We also meet her family and Dr. Helene Quaile, a physician Anna had consulted for school physicals and various other medical reasons.

Anna remarks:

> *"Of course, I did not know at the time, that the day would be the first in a long, long journey, one that would uncover one of the most bizarre fates that life had to offer: an expedition into the world of doctors and the system that governs their profession."*

CHAPTER 2

A Visit with Iris

Anna meets her friend Iris—a medical assistant in Dr. Quaile's office—for lunch. Iris tells Anna that a hospital is in the process of acquiring Dr. Quaile's practice to lessen the increasing burden of paperwork triggered by third-party reimbursements. The doctor, who is suffering from what looks like burnout, might not be able to continue to practice. Iris is a faithful employee, and patients and companies appreciate the services offered by the medical office.

During this conversation, Anna is confronted by the deterioration of the healthcare system. The new reimbursement puzzles harm primary care doctors' already reduced salaries. Furthermore, she begins to see the emergence of suspicion by insurances companies that doctors are felons for overbilling for services. She witnesses the pervasive impact of this suspicion on trusting employees and on the morale of the whole office. Since Anna's future spouse is in medical school, she is rightfully concerned.

The media is blaming physicians for the increasing cost of healthcare and pointing fingers at doctors as if they were criminals who overcharged for services. However, providers' fees account for an insignificant eight percent of the U.S. total medical costs. The country is becoming progressively more legalistic and bureaucratic, and the future of the entire medical profession seems bleak.

Anna does not perceive Dr. Quaile's office to be high risk. The staff seems diligent and meticulous about the care of everyone coming through the door.

CHAPTER 3

Dr. Helene Quaile

Dr. Quaile appears to be a dedicated and reserved woman who fought her own personal battle to attend medical school. Initially, she struggled against gender inequality and asserted her wishes to be a doctor. She appears to live a modest life -- not what one would expect. Dr. Quaile does not belong to the stereotype of high-paid physicians.

The doctor writes some personal notes about hassles the office faces. These are not difficulties of medical diagnosis, but of insurance payments and measures to prevent petty collection issues. Doctors charge for time with a patient but are not paid for all additional time reviewing lab results, doing reports, overseeing other doctors, and managing a practice. As the practice grows, the doctor not only is faced with increasing overhead but also an increasing unpaid personal workload.

Then there's the added complexity of dealing with problem patients. Enter John Pasternak, who will play a major role later in the book. After receiving a request for all his medical records from a personal injury attorney, the doctor suspects that he is working with an attorney who is an ambulance chaser. She had been suspicious about this patient but now realizes that something is extremely wrong about his actions and frequent visits to other doctors in the practice. She does not suspect that he is suing for malpractice, but rather that he is creating a medical record to claim injuries for a recent accident using a former injury of a foot fracture. She decides to discharge him from the practice. From these notes, it's clear that the medical office is not involved in filing worker's compensation cases but in preventing them.

CHAPTER 4

Rashōmon

This chapter introduces an important conundrum about aspects and risks of criminalization. Anna has a class studying the movie that gave the name to the legal term: the Rashomon effect.

Anna observes: *"I realized that Rashōmon was perhaps the finest movie ever to investigate the philosophy of justice … the relationship between subjectivity, perception, and recollection. The idea that observers of an event are able to produce substantially different but equally plausible accounts of a story seemed fascinating to me. If verbal recounting is as subjective, why are we relying on it so heavily?"*

Anna deals with an example of the Rashomon effect when her fiancé, Paul, and his surgical team are blamed for not keeping a patient alive even though they resuscitated the patient multiple times before determining that he could not live.

It's clear that the justice system faces contradictory testimonies built on personal biases and preconceptions. In Paul's case, the patient's family assumed that he should have lived because he was in a hospital. On the other hand, doctors were confronted with the reality of a seriously injured patient with arterial damage beyond repair.

CHAPTER 5

Iris

Dr. Quaile's practice has been around for a long time and is well regarded. It is under contracts with corporations in the city of Dakota to meet employees' daily healthcare needs. Companies appreciate the office's worker's compensation prevention and its efforts to fight fraud and false claims. The practice also faces security issues, like the drug dealer attempting to insinuate himself into the office.

Iris gives more details on the deeper changes that third party reimbursements have caused. Besides the additional paperwork for both, providers and payers, insurance clerks are often disrespectful of the medical staff. This affects Iris, as third party payers are disrupting the once simple process. This also leaves a gap for patients to potentially take advantage. It appears as if the efforts spent by insurance companies to decrease medical costs, in actuality appear to increase the practice operating. These measures also drive a wedge between patients and medical staff. This causes increasing resentments and often disrupts patient care. Insurance companies are prompting patients to suspect doctors of fraud; and the staff is upset at being distrusted. Lastly, additional clerical and management costs affect doctors' bottom line.

Part II

Physician's Oath

"I will practice my profession with conscience and dignity; the health of my patient will be my first consideration."

Part II will uncover why the doctor disappeared and how criminalization may be misused and harmful to solving healthcare expenditures.

CHAPTER 7

A Lawyer's Talk

Anna consults with an attorney she occasionally meets in town over coffee. She picks her brain about legal procedures and requirements for due process. She is appalled by her lawyer friend's casual manner in addressing the professional responsibility for notice of pending hearing or what is also called "due process." She begins to realize how readily a defendant could also fail to receive an adverse outcome to a legal case. Moreover, the attorney sows doubt on Dr. Quaile's appearance of honesty rather than offering reassurance. The attorney appears convinced of a judge's ability to recognize improprieties or transgressions by prosecutors and their witnesses.

Anna's doubts about the justice system grow. She believes that her friend is oblivious to her new perception that the system is working against physicians and railroading innocents. It fuels her determination to investigate. Skepticism is overtaking her view of the legal profession, prosecutors, and the overall efficiency of the system.

CHAPTER 8

Research

Anna studies the doctor's hearing transcript in more detail. She also spends more time on the due process requirements to understand why the doctor did not offer a defense. In reviewing reports of similar actions against other doctors, it appears that many doctors are accused of the same infractions: filing false reports, providing excessive treatment, or conducting fraudulent practice by failing to maintain adequate records. She also finds cases of doctors who are allegedly drug dealers as well as cases of older physicians whose licenses have been suspended or revoked for annoying patients. She also finds that the AMA is concerned about the increasing intrusion of the government into medical care.

Since Anna knows that Dr. Quaile was a victim of fraud by a few patients, she cannot imagine how these instances could have been turned around so that the doctor became the perpetrator of the fraud. It seems inconsistent with what Anna has witnessed of her husband in medical school followed by his arduous training. Most studies show that mental illnesses, negligence due to burnout, and addiction should be of concern to authorities, not whether they are felons. On the other hand, she learns that at one point the Department of Health was accused of inducing restaurants to bribe officials for license approval and begins to wonder if the cause for the harsh treatment is that these doctors might have refused to pay an inducement. She learns of a federal decision made in 1993 to fight fraud and about approaches used to do so. In licensing statistic reports, she observes a sharp increase in the cases of misconduct and license revocations. The number of prosecuted physicians has almost doubled from 1997 to the present. Anna determines that there is one prosecutor for every 300 physicians. She realizes that if the process continues, this could affect access to healthcare in the whole country.

CHAPTER 9

Tom Nesh

Tom Nesh is the prosecutor for this case. He shares his job's function and personal point of view on his role in disciplining physicians. His work is derived from a direct order from the White House to Governors, Attorney General, and Commissioner of Health to decrease healthcare expenditures. His impression is that doctors are the reason for the high cost of healthcare, and that they need to be controlled to change the situation. His position and future depend on the success of these efforts. Tom Nesh does not seem to be very concerned about the means but rather the end. He admits to being a little bit lax about due process procedures. He may also have a few personal vendettas. He believes that his ability to control doctors' licenses gives him a lot of power. He further brags about tactics he uses to win cases and appears to be an employee who just follows procedures whether they make sense or are ethical.

In the first hearing against Dr. Helen Quaile, the judge and Tom Nesh debate at length about the due process procedures. The prosecutor states he has done all needed to reach the defendant claiming that she is "hiding from the law," but the judge does not agree. Eventually, the hearing is adjourned. Following the hearing, Tom meets with an old friend and former colleague. From their conversion, it's clear Tom may have a personal vendetta against a doctor who refused to pay him a sum of money he requested.

CHAPTER 10

Due Process

Anna studies the first hearing record of the three sessions and tries to understand what went wrong with the "due process."

The prosecutor says a UPS mailing as well as a process server served an address where the doctor was unknown. Anna also notes that, despite the failed attempt, all subsequent documents were still sent to the erroneous address.

The hearing occurred two years after the doctor stopped practicing. In Anna's phone call to the office, she obtained the doctor's address without any problems. She had also received notice of it as a patient of the practice. Anna also obtains the same address from the Department of Education, where licensing records are kept. It is different from the one used by the prosecutor.

In the hearing, the prosecutor blames the doctor for not updating her address. It is unclear why she should contact him to update him of any personal moves. Could the statement relate to the money he is referring to in the conversation with his friend in the previous chapter? The implication is clear: why should the doctor have to pay the prosecutor? He claims he has satisfied the requirements and presents the doctor as someone running from the law, stating, "It's obvious in this case the doctor herself deliberately failed to inform us of her new address."

Anna also discovers that the probable cause for this is that the requirements for "due process" are to show proof of service to the last known address. There are no requirements to prove that the address is "registered" or current. Returned mail and certification by a process server in this case apparently established that the person does not live at that address and that the defendant is "running from the law." In reality, Anna is able to reach the doctor, who told her that she just received an official letter announcing the revocation of the license but with no reason given. This is three months after the end of the third and last hearing. This established that the prosecutor did have her correct home address. It also has set up a situation in which the doctor is unable to appeal the decision because the time to do that has elapsed.

Dr. Quaile hired an attorney (Tom Nesh's friend) regarding an investigation after she stopped practicing. She ended the relationship when the attorney requested $60,000 on behalf of the prosecutor to cease the inquiry. This new fact clarifies the vendetta Tom Nesh might have against the defendant. The doctor states that she refused to pay, as she wasn't aware of any wrongdoing and subsequently never received any official correspondence.

CHAPTER 11

Judge Steven Masden

The judge presents his views and details of the second hearing. He is astounded by how many charges are on that list and the serious nature of the transgressions: defrauding insurance, fee splitting, and racketeering? He states, "This woman must be a real felon. Let's see what Nesh brings forth; he must have evidences."

The second hearing reveals that the prosecutor met the requirements for "due process." The hearing is held without the presence of a defense. The judge, however, is perturbed and comments again, "Everyone in the profession of law knows that when a defendant is absent, you only hear half of the story. Most courts would never allow this state of affairs. It is an important civil right. The right to present a defense is constitutionally guaranteed." Continuing on, the prosecutor presents a first witness, a physician. The witness agrees with most allegations. Other members of board for the hearing ask similar questions that implicate the doctor. Since no defense is present, the judge offers a defense side in his private comments. The one-sided negative presentation of Dr. Quaile is evident. The prosecutor presents every imaginable allegation, including fraud, inadequate medical records, and billing issues. Later in the story, it comes to light that he tampered with his evidences to make his points.

CHAPTER 12

A Visit in Dakota

Anna's father is a professor of political science at a renowned college. They discuss the case over lunch. Anna has researched a witness from the second hearing, an older doctor in his eighties. She has found discrepancies in his reported background that appears to disguise his actual age. This point brings up the issue of whether this witness is appropriate for such an important decision.

Anna's father confirms her suspicions and calls the process a "malicious peer review." He points out that in hospitals, doctors who are standing up for patients' rights have been known to be the subject of such reviews. Anna shows her father part of the hearing documentation regarding claims of incomplete medical history by the doctor. She explains that these are very inconsistent with what she knows of the doctor's performance. It looks as if the prosecutors shared only part of the complete detailed reports the doctor was known for, and that Anna had received as a patient of the practice.

In summary, the impression she receives from her father is that the lack of due process is the most predominant failure in this case, which in turn, results in the prosecutor exploiting his one-man show.

CHAPTER 13

Dr. Quaile's Notes

Anna collates some of Dr. Quaile's notes, which relate the doctor's personal suffering when she learns of the hearings and reads the results. Apart from the fact that she is recovering from an illness, the hearings affect her physically and mentally. She suffers from insomnia, intense headaches, and personal inner torment. She relates feeling extremely confused, as if she had been poisoned, and on being on the brink of suicide from the exhaustion caused by loss of sleep.

We also witness the cold treatment she received from the Medical Society, where she had been very active. It is as if everyone is afraid of being associated with her because of the outcome of the hearings. She is recommended to a law firm, which surrenders quickly and states that no one can fight the King, (the licensing authorities). Moreover, the cost of a lawsuit would be over $200,000.

It is becoming evident that law firms she contacts are afraid of state authorities; Dr. Quaile sees a parallel with the Salem Witch Trials. There is also a parallel with the reaction of victims of rape and the shame they suffer.

Anna is profoundly touched and upset by these notes. She feels strongly as if this is an example scapegoating healthcare issues onto good physicians. Further, she uncovers additional issues with witnesses that she needs to investigate.

CHAPTER 14

Pasternak Under Oath

Anna reviews the third hearing. She discovers that the additional witnesses used by Tom Nesh are patients that Dr. Quaile had discharged for dishonesty. The prosecutor makes misleading arguments that overstate the probative value of the findings. He presents the doctor as a racketeer, a Medicaid mill forcing patients to have unnecessary tests and charging for unperformed procedures. His behavior is cited as typical misconduct seen in many of The Innocence Project cases.

In this third and last hearing, the doctor again is absent because of the prosecutor's failure to reach her. She receives information in March—more than three months after this last session. It's so close to the appeal deadline that the doctor is unable to appeal. The first witness in this hearing is the patient Dr. Quaile suspected of filing false claims. The prosecutor is clearly relying on a fraudulent witness.

The testimony is aimed at blaming the doctor for the witness's larceny. The prosecutor is observed in additional misconduct such as: allowing witnesses they know are not truthful to testify and making gross overstatements on allegations that the doctor is running a racketeering operation.

Anna finds many more obvious discrepancies in the accusations. From the medical records she received from the doctor, she uncovers that they are discussing a shoulder X-Ray when the chart contains only a foot X-Ray. She can see that the actual foot X-Ray would not have been good since it disclosed the actual fraud the patient was intending -- that is, passing off an old fracture as a new one to obtain compensation for an accident in which he did not get hurt or sustain any injuries. This is not unintentional oversight, but a situation that establishes the actual intent by Tom Nesh to falsify evidence. It also points to the obliviousness or possible colluding of the board attending this hearing.

In the witness's records, Anna finds very few visits by Dr. Quaile. She finds reports of numerous walk-in visits for accidents, gastrointestinal issues, and other subjects. The witness describes three separate accidents with taxis. Following that, it seems as if with each visit he scheduled, he attempted to run a large medical bill to create evidence of medical cost. Anna does not find any notes from the doctor confirming that she had ordered any of the alleged tests, except for those that were essential to a routine assessment.

The rest of the hearing is more of the same, full of confusing nonfactual allegations. There is no substantial proof of what is advanced by the witness. Members of the board interrogate the witness, who continues a rant of defense and hearsay for his cause.

Finally, Anna analyzes the witness's motives. She evaluates the cost of the medical care requested to be about $22,000. The patient intended to receive compensation from the taxi company that he claimed hit him. Additionally, he received reimbursement from two separate insurances since he had two employers. Both of these felonies could have put the witness behind bars.

CHAPTER 15

An Unexpected Surprise

Anna gets a reprieve from the arduous hearings and leaves for a trip to Canada with her husband. Nonetheless, she has discussions about the Canadian Healthcare system.

CHAPTER 16

Burr Under Oath

In this chapter, we are again visiting the third hearing. A new witness is under oath. We heard of Jen Burr in a prior chapter. In chapter 6 we saw how she forced her way into the doctor's office pretending to be ill to get a routine check-up. Subsequently, her dishonest conduct, bad credit card, and checks, cause her to receive a discharge from the office.

We witness, once more, the prosecutor allowing a deceitful witness to testify. In actuality, court searches reveal that Jen Burr is currently behind bars, and long lists of legal cases follow her name. These cases present her rather as a sociopath than an actress. The prosecutor continues to misapply evidence deliberately and make disingenuous (misleading) arguments overstating the probative value of testimony. For example, he uses the past medical history of the witness to fabricate a list of current medical history (presenting complaints). The witness is lying under oath. She is claiming that the doctor billed for unperformed procedures. This allegation is impossible since the results from a laboratory and other digital forms and date stamp.

In this chapter, one can observe, in details, the abiding of the misconduct by the entire board. They fail to notice the discrepancies between the witness statements and the medical records. The prosecutor would have had to withhold the particular witness's chart. In fact, not only do they looks at the records discussed but also interrogate the witness. Her testimony is inconsistent and aimed at disparage the doctor she conveniently used to obtain a free check-up.

Despite those inconsistencies in records, the prosecutor and witness successfully convinced the board that the doctor has created false diagnoses. They rehash her list of past medical history noted in her chart, asking the witness whether she complained of these issues. Indeed, it appears as if the patient did not complain of these symptoms, but reported them in the medical history filled out in her handwriting.

This chapter points to misapplication of pieces of evidence and failure of due process.

CHAPTER 17

Carol & Jeff

Anna reviews other cases brought by the state and covered by the media, including that of an infertility doctor who adjusted billing or diagnoses codes to deal with a lack of reimbursement for particular procedures. The law was modified to address the issue the infertility physician was trying to circumvent. However, the physician was convicted. The court ruled that his bending codes to address a patient's coverage issues were against the law. His patients had considered him a hero, but they were not responsible for the restitution for the infertility treatments to the insurance company. The doctor is sentenced to five years in jail and fined millions of dollars in restitution. Opinions on the case are divided. Some feel that insurance companies were at fault; others believe the verdict is just. Should the patient have paid back the insurance company or the doctor, since they benefited from his care? Who should decide what the ethical level of treatment is—the doctor, the patient, the government, or the insurance company?

Are those proceedings really about addressing the cost of healthcare, since doctors' fees represent only a tiny percentage of the total cost? At the same time, Anna notes many well-known cases of primary care physicians who cannot make enough to survive in practice. She also remarks that the aggressive legal approach of pursuing doctors does not address citizens' increasing expectations of care, sophisticated technology, or fears of malpractice by providers.

In another case, an attorney defended a patient who brought tapes as proof of sexual abuse by a therapist. The attorney is aware that the evidence is weak but hopes that the malpractice insurance will buckle and pay.

Anna wonders if the current situation is similar to the Salem Witch Trials. Is the hunt similar, failing to search for solutions to a much more complex issue?

CHAPTER 18

Kristin "About Ms. Burr"

Kristin, the manager of Dr. Quaile's office, tells the account of Ms. Burr. Many of the facts were explained in Chapter 6, but this is a second account describing the frustrating experience that someone who had to manage the issues of patients had encountered with Ms. Burr's dishonesty.

CHAPTER 19

Mount Sterling, PA

Now back to the present, Anna locates Dr. Quaile, who has moved to another state and is living on a very modest farm. The doctor has tried repeatedly to be heard by authorities, but to no avail. She's only succeeded in subjecting herself to being sued by the prosecutor for one million dollars for libel. The vulnerability of the medical profession is clear. The doctor's efforts to follow the license restoration path recommended by the state causes her more financial losses and distress. While she courageously faces every committee appointed to her case, the authorities and the commissioner have no interest in resolving the misconduct and its costly consequences. The commissioner says, as the meeting ends, "We hear your concerns, but it is not our position to change what happened."

Anna describes the story of the medical profession and how the government has impacted healthcare in dangerous ways by decimating the occupation of an estimated 100,000 physicians. While the government's concept may have been well intended to address the rising cost of healthcare, the means used have caused severe damage and have not addressed the real causes of the rise in healthcare costs. The commissioner does not take action after Dr. Quaile uses costly legal procedures to address the misconduct. This outcome does not produce much confidence in the people overseeing professionals and their unjust prosecutions, leaving Anna with profound doubts. Since Anna still can't find a doctor, she wonders if the intended goal of the government was to revoke licenses in order to cause shortages that would, in turn, decrease total medical costs.

CHAPTER 20

Small Victories

A small victory comes when Anna meets a prosecutor from the U.S. Department of Health & Human Services at a family baptism. The conversation confirms one of her suspicions about why the government is prosecuting physicians rather than other entities such as medical suppliers or hospitals.

The prosecutor reveals that doctors are fruitful monetary targets, because hospitals are loaded with defense attorneys. He shares that the principal objective of his department is reclaiming money as the dollar amount proves to the public that it is where the problem lies and that is the proof that government is finding a solution. Essentially, the government is robbing Peter to pay Paul, perpetrating a witch-hunt against physicians.

The admission by the prosecutor is one small victory for Anna, who continues to strive to understand the unfair punishment. Now she has uncovered one of the roots of the issue.

Conclusion

The national effort to target the medical profession began when the Clinton administration introduced the concept of "Healthcare offenses" into the general public lexicon in the 1993 "Health Security Act."

Gene Healy from the Cato Institute raised concerns of whether excessive reliance on punishment can increase harm. He pointed to the draconian approaches being adopted as discouraging physicians.

"Lumping trivial with serious transgressions undermines people's sense of morality." He continued by pointing out that "the lack of clarity in the laws and the immense bureaucratic discretion to define standards create serious risks of corruption." Healy maintained that rather than address the issues at stake, it "will provide new business opportunities for those particularly skilled in these arts."

Healy stated, "Courts should be more protective of common law rights and constitutional principles. Rules that are not ascertainable after reasonable effort should be enforced only by a cease-and-desist order, not by civil or criminal penalties."

In the example of Dr. Quaile, there were no intentional deceits. She appears to have followed and complied diligently with new regulations; she was not negligent in any legal or moral sense.

Nancy Dickey, M.D., former president of the American Medical Association pointed out that "demonizing the entire medical community with a broad brush of 'fraud, waste and abuse' trivializes real fraud and sets an adversarial tension in every patient-physician encounter."

Grace-Marie Turner, president of the Galen Institute, in an article entitled "HIPAA and the Criminalization of American Medicine," noted that: "an expanding dragnet for 'healthcare criminals' is threatening and intimidating innocent doctors as well." Turner also stated that, "in its zeal to rid the nation's healthcare system of waste, fraud, and abuse, Congress has passed a blizzard of new federal criminal provisions targeting the Healthcare Industry."

Turner goes on to say, "Statutes are enforced by hundreds of federal agents, armed with hundreds of millions of dollars in investigatory funds. The new army of law enforcement agents has been sweeping through hospitals and doctor's offices throughout the country to investigate a new class of 'healthcare offenders.' The federal government uses the threat of prosecution and arbitrary penalties to collect excessive settlements from doctors 'guilty' of clerical errors."

Marion Stahl stipulated, "It's evident that the idea of being a criminal does not enter most physician's mind. It is a foreign idea reserved for school dropouts not common among high achievers. This detail took doctors off guard and increased their intrinsic vulnerability."

Turner states, "Most of HIPAA's fraud and abuse provisions were passed despite the absence of good data on how much fraud and abuse there is, where it is, and how bad it is." Congressional policy toward healthcare fraud was fueled by political polls, which in turn, were fed by misinformation and crude political expediency, or the vague need to "do something about waste, fraud, and abuse." Turner explained,

"There is a misconception that high healthcare costs are almost exclusively the result of fraud. Political leaders failed to educate the public on the seriousness of Medicare's financial problems. Stopping every instance of fraud and improper billing could not come close to saving Medicare from its looming insolvency. While Congress and the Clinton administration engaged in a scam and abuse vendetta, both did an abysmal job of reforming a government system that remains a greenhouse for corruption. Clearly, it is easier for politicians to point fingers at doctors than to blame themselves for the flawed public policies that created the climate for waste in the healthcare system in the first place."

Dr. Robert Waller, Chair Emeritus of the Mayo Foundation and former president of the Healthcare Leadership Council, told the National Bipartisan Commission on the Future of Medicare that, "Regulatory complexity, rather than widespread fraud in the program, is the real problem."

AMA President Daniel Johnson, M.D. stated, "Why not be on the side of trying to get this fixed rather than throwing hundreds of millions of dollars at these investigations?"

Additional Reading:

A Monster Chase, Summary & Analysis by US Legal Research

Analysis

After reading this story, readers yearn for a resolution not given by this book. The author intends to sensitize the reader to a current problematic situation in healthcare. This book describes the experience of a young woman who takes it upon herself to investigate the reason for the shortage of physicians. We hear of only one doctor but become aware that many are accused of fraud. The author uses Anna's character to analyze the process and pressing issues in prosecutions.

The narrator brings readers into a medical practice and, eventually, the ultimate results of aggressive prosecutorial approach. We witness the impact not only on employees but also on the overall healthcare system and the resulting significant damages to the medical profession.

The author does not exclude the possibility that there are troubled doctors but questions whether the current disciplinary approach has worked. She shows how the guilty could easily buy their way out with the current method. The criminalization approach has damaged trust in the medical profession, discouraged providers as well as eliminated many, and failed to resolve the financial concerns. In this vein, malpractice has resulted in much abuse and created a generation that blames rather than solves real problems, such as doctor burnout and improvement of hospital team management. Rather than addressing and correcting underlying issues, we believe that by pointing fingers at individuals or professions, we will solve a much larger problem. The author shows the shortsightedness of the approach and its failure. The overreach by government and negative results need a solution.

This book sensitizes the reader to a reality different from what is claimed by government reports. The United States healthcare financial crisis cannot be resolved by revoking licenses, asking retributions and display results. It is a satisfaction for justice that will not last. In reality, physicians' fees represent a minuscule part of total cost. If we revoked the licenses of all providers in the US, we would only solve 8% of the total annual healthcare costs in the US and would create a nightmare. Hence, we have not achieved much since the most important culprit of the cost lies in our change in expectations of care.

The Author's Positions:

1. Disciplining physicians will not resolve our healthcare financial crisis. It has created another crisis: a shortage of doctors.
2. DNA analysis has proven that our troubled justice system is punishing innocents. This story shows well-intended professionals, not only death row inmates, can become victims of the system.

Together the points made in this book are simple.

We always imagine doctors have power and fail to realize their vulnerability. The author recognized that the profession has not been in control of the press and needed a new side to the story.

Given the current beliefs (that physicians are at the root of the problem), readers need to hear a real story to understand.

In summary, readers will learn about a serious issue. Current reports have given the false impression that addressing physician fraud would resolve the healthcare financial crisis. In actuality, it appears that it has caused a new, more serious one and delayed needed action. The use of scapegoating is not unusual, yet it only soothes short-term emotional anxiety and delays real solutions.

We see that excessive reliance on punishment can actually increase harm. As Gene Healy, from the Cato Institute, points out in his research, "Overuse of punitive sanction damages the moral fabric of the culture."

Legal Aspects and Comments:

This story has several facets. It addresses the issues and complications of over criminalization of medicine but also addresses some of the shortcoming of our justice system as well. The author used Anna and the judge's voice to show various aspects of misconduct.

1. Tainted evidence: the prosecutor shows incomplete records and presents partial lab results as proof of fraud.

2. Misleading arguments: Confusing the witness with unclear questions with incomplete records to prompt a desired answer.

3. Overstating the probative value of the findings: We also see the thin line in the forms of accusation between simple billing errors and fraud. There is no proof that there was any intentional deceit, but the prosecutor presents it as such to sway members of the board for the hearing toward his goal.

The innocence project lists the following are common forms of misconduct by prosecutors:

1. Withholding exculpatory evidence from the defense.

2. Deliberately mishandling, mistreating, or destroying evidence.

3. Allowing witnesses they know or should know are not truthful to testify.

4. Pressuring defense witnesses not to testify.

5. Relying on fraudulent forensic experts.

6. Making misleading arguments that overstate the probative value of testimony.

Many of these misconducts are observed in these hearings.

In these hearings one observes:

<u>Problematic Due Process:</u>

In this book, and hearings, one observes how easily the responsibility of notice or due process is circumvented on many occasions.

Misapplication of pieces of evidence:

In a similar way, a prosecutor may use a bloodstain from another source and use it as proof of murder. Here, we observe the prosecutor using a different set of questions routinely asked of patients during their initial visit about their past medical history. He uses this as evidence of 'current problem' and deceives trained professional in believing that they are evidence that the doctor is at fault. In actuality, they are the annoying questionnaire every doctor requires at first visit we all know. This misapplication of proof achieves the goal of misleading the listener into believing that the physician intended to defraud the insurance with a 'kangaroo court' approach.

We observe the prosecutor misusing a set of questions routinely asked of patients during their initial visit about their past medical history. This becomes evidence that the doctor used past medical history to indicate current problems and treatments of a patient. This achieves the goal to support allegations but really deceives any listener into believing that the doctor is at fault. In reality, this set of questions is simply the annoying questionnaire we are all familiar with and required at every doctor's first visit. Any physician trained in medical school is taught to request this information. If one were to make this argument, the only doctors who would avoid the wrath of this prosecutor would be negligent physicians.

What is described here is the equivalent of a prosecutor using a bloodstain from one location as proof of murder in another location. This misapplication of proof achieves the goal of misleading the listener into believing that the physician intended to defraud the insurance. It is an example of a "kangaroo court" approach or a more likely, a blatant disregard of standard law and justice.

Problematic Witnesses:

Finally, in the same manner, the first patient witness had attempted to protect himself against legal repercussions of what he had committed, this new witness motive is to seek protection by blaming the practice to avoid the potential consequence of her dishonest and fraudulent actions

We observe the use of tainted evidence or information created to sway the verdict in a court case. Finally, the defendant is made to look guilty rather than thanked for giving Good Samaritan services and fighting fraud but rather demonized as a doctor running a test mill.

Discussion on Medical Boards:

The importance of physicians being involved in such proceedings has been debated for a hundred year. However, we can see how Medical Board Member with little prosecutorial experience can be swayed easily in such situation and failed to recognize how their colleague was railroaded in being accused of being a criminal. Do state-run institutions with little knowledge of medicine achieve disciplining professions best? Would a Medical Organization such as the Federation of Medical Board not better equipped and capable of doing this job?

It seems as if the focus of such proceedings might be more productive if focused on learning issues that cause errors. Using an approach to attempt to correct such errors rather than blaming would be productive and confer a reliable support for the profession rather than cause the current alienation. In the story, Dr. Quaile is never given a chance to have a conversation with anyone about the allegations the State has 'uncovered'. It appears as if there are no attempts to look at the actual situation but rather use witnesses with questionable accusations to make a point about overspending in healthcare. If every state board acts in a similar way, it is not surprising that we have a shortage of providers. Physicians have lost faith and moved on. Is that what we want?

Criminalization of Professional Mistakes:

Attorneys are in charge of most of State Boards, not physicians trained in healthcare policy. In extensive research, Sidney W.A. Dekker, Professor at School of Humanities at Griffith University and author of several books on the subject investigates the issues of criminology and values of prosecuting for professional errors rather than investigate their causes. He states: "The criminalization of professional mistake may represent a jurisprudential meaning-making (Jacobs & Henry, 1996; Phillips & Grattet, 2000)." He continues with: "The same issues are seen in the airline industry. Most fields of safety-critical practice express concern about the prosecution of professional mistake." The significant aspect of this debate is that as we fail to learn from failures and hamper progress. Rather than addressing the cause and prevent reoccurrences, it appears easier to blame and move on.

Conclusion:

Aside from the questionable value of using criminalization to deal with professional mistakes, the human and problematic moral of the story is that such flawed proceedings could happen to anyone in any settings.

This publication was supported
by a grant from
US Legal Research

Made in the USA
Monee, IL
04 November 2026

67386113R10036